Millennial Spring

Eight New Oregon Poets

Millennial Spring

Eight New Oregon Poets

Edited by Peter Sears
& Michael Malan

Cloudbank Books
Corvallis, Oregon

© by Peter Sears and Michael Malan. All rights reserved.

This book, or any part thereof, may not be reproduced by any means, written or mechanical, or be programmed into any electronic retrieval or information storage system, without expressed written permission from the publisher, except for short passages for purpose of review.

First Edition 2 3 4 5 6 7 8 9

Library of Congress Cataloging in Publication Data

Sears, Peter, 1937 –
      Millennial Spring

ISBN 0-936085-42-8

Cloudbank Books is an imprint of
Blue Heron Books, Portland, Oregon

To Wilma Erwin
poetry activist, community activist

Contents

### Introduction	1

### Susan Spady	6

Carrying Eggs; Underpants; Wishing Pool; Child of Somalia; Practice This Ending; Last Day; Bruised; Grief; Pretending; Flower Leaning from a Vase

### Victoria Wyttenberg	18

Flowers Have Beauty and Roots Have Worth; Curve and Connection; The School Photographer; Imprecation Against Adultery; House for Sale; Bird Shadows; The Curse; Blueberries; Blue Heron; For My Oldest Child

### Charles Goodrich	32

Millennial Spring; The Insects of South Corvallis; Heavenly Bodies; Hover Fly; Stinging Nettles

### Barbara Davis	46

Come Together Down the Canyon Where It Was Good; Conversation in the Dark; The Artist at Fifty-One; Why the One-Eyed Yellow Dog; One Syllable Villanelle; The Bloom of Gold Needles; Chamber Work for the Eighth Day; Hills the Glacier Left Us; Paper Nautilus; The Explanation of Acorns; Persimmons; In the Garden of the Women; The Blue Angel Raphael Breaks His Silence to Explain

### Debra Brimacombe	60

Breakfast Bites; High Desert; Spans; Simply Taught; Before They Can Hang Up; Debra's Oak Tree; Intersection; When the Flag Was Raised Over the Hugh Whitson Memorial Elementary School (Back When It Was Called White Salmon Elementary School); Autumn's Eaten Apple; Swallows; Take, Hold; Alone

Harold Johnson 72

Stealing the Shortstop's Shoes; The Names of Summer: A War Memory; Water Pitcher; And You, Gilbert Stuart; Private Birdsong Speaks; Smell Theory; At the Jackson Pollock Retrospective in L.A.

Pat Ware 84

Death, The Helium Eye; Permission for Autopsy; Obligations of Solitude; Long Beach; An Apostle's Greed; Listening to Distance; Calling Out Light; Immolation; Flukefish; The Loner; The Window over St. Vincent Garden; Theresa; How Deep is the Garden?

Carolyn Miller 98

The Curved Lens of Forgetting; The Girl Who Loved Groceries; Fugue in Green; Salt Lick; Ma Bête; Piscatorial Longing; Spinning; Falling Forward into Light

Credits 112

INTRODUCTION

To get one's poems published, while it has never been easy in this country, has become even more difficult it seems, especially for new poets, as fewer publishing houses maintain a stable of poets, small-press distributors cannot stay afloat, and Congress has crippled the National Endowment for the Arts.

Co-editor Michael Malan and I, discussing this problem, found ourselves wanting to do something for Northwest poets. We considered starting a magazine. I balked at all the reading. We could take submissions by invitation only, Michael suggested. That sounded better. We could draw good submissions by invitation; I was thinking of the many capable poets in writing workshops of mine here in Oregon.

Some years ago, Sandra McPherson told me that she found promising poets in her workshop teaching. She is a popular poet and teacher here in Oregon, even though she has moved away and has lived in California for many years. I mentioned to Michael what Sandra McPherson had said to me, and he and I talked further about publishing new voices in Northwest poetry.

We pulled back from the Northwest, figuring we could secure enough good work just in Oregon. We dropped our idea of a magazine in favor of a set of chapbooks. We would look for five poets and do chapbooks of 20 pages of poetry each. To focus on poets with the least exposure, we decided to confine our invitations to poets with neither a book nor a chapbook. Our best opportunity to contribute, we thought, was on behalf of new poets. That was fine as long as we received good poems. So we would encourage the invited poets to send as many poems as they wished. Some would have book manuscripts. We would have much to choose from.

I got word out to poets who had been in workshops of mine and who might have a wide range of poems. Four of these poets are in the book: Carolyn Miller, Barbara Davis, Pat Ware, and Debra Brimacombe. Meanwhile, Michael contacted Susan Spady here in Corvallis. Barbara Davis was first to recommend Harold Johnson, and Carolyn Miller and Susan Spady recommended Victoria Wyttenberg. Rich Wandschneider, director of Fishtrap in Eastern Oregon, said a highlight of the workshop the past summer had been the work of Charles Goodrich. We invited Charles.

These eight were among the original group of 20 poets invited to submit. The more we read the work of the 20 poets and talked about it, the more convinced we became that we did not have an obvious five poets. Once we started thinking seven, eight, nine poets, we thought of an anthology, which we saw as doing better perhaps than chapbooks in bookstores and libraries. Chapbooks don't fare well in Oregon bookstores, it appears, unless they are displayed face out, a rare sight. We settled on an anthology of eight poets of 12 to 14 pages per poet. This goodly number of pages made for the poet's largest publication of poems to date. This was our intent.

Soon we realized we would help ourselves considerably were we to bring in a third reader. Ann Staley, co-founding editor of *Fireweed*, a literary magazine of the Willamette Valley, accepted our invitation to serve as associate editor. We gave her the eight poets' submissions, noted our selections, and asked her to evaluate our work. This request led to vibrant discussions over lunch at the Valley Restaurant here in Corvallis. Ann has had a major hand in rounding out the selections of the eight poets.

The three of us editors were surprised by our high degree of consensus in selecting each poet's work. I thought I would cause a snag because I am leery of Oregon's strong preference for narrative poetry, and we received a lot of it from our invited poets. The strength of Oregon poetry may very well be its clarity, its accessibility; and the narrative bent contributes to this clarity. But a clarity of another sort may be the weakness of Oregon poetry. A prosiness often taking the form of a personal narrative makes for a snapshot poetry. This sort of thing crops up in workshops in such a comment as "But that's what really happened." Here in Oregon, many personal recollections are passed off as poems. To meld the two takes a fine poet.

These eight new Oregon poets work in narrative poetry to varying degrees. We editors believe their narrative poems here are strong. Which is not to say the poets wouldn't benefit from experimenting more with voice, diction, and traditional forms. For each poet, we tried to select a representative group of poems. We made a few editorial suggestions, primarily lines they might drop, but we did not attach a condition of revision to accepting a poem.

When we conceived of publishing new Oregon poets, my first thought was of the benefit we had in Michael Malan's twenty-five years in publishing newspapers and magazines. When we decided to do an anthology, my first thought was of *Five Poets of the Pacific Northwest* from University of Washington Press in 1964. This was the book by which I first came to know Northwest poetry. I loved the book then, and still do. Robin Shelton's selection of poets—Kenneth O. Hanson, Richard Hugo, Carolyn Kizer, William Stafford, and David Wagoner—and their poems is proving, over the years, to be truly impressive. Often I brought the book along to our editorial lunches.

Surely, *Five Poets of the Pacific Northwest* is the yardstick for Northwest poetry anthologies. A publisher of a new anthology risks having his or her book compared to this 1964 anthology. This association is fine with us, though. Our "New Oregon Poets" are not well known. They haven't published a book of poems. But they do look to the "Five Poets of the Pacific Northwest," and some of them say so in describing their own writing in their anthology introductions.

Of the "Five Poets of the Pacific Northwest," all but one of them were students of Theodore Roethke. Moreover, most of the poets stayed and taught in the Northwest, creating for the region a kind of instructional ballast and cultural literacy. Arguably, were it not for their work, there might not have been, in 1993, the Oregon Literature Series, from the Oregon Council of Teachers of English and published by Oregon State University Press. The six-volume series demonstrates that writing of genuine stature has been going on in the Northwest for a long time. The Oregon Literature Series is a bridge from the non-white cultures settling the Northwest to the mixing of peoples of the present. Four of the eight poets in this book are also in the Oregon Literature Series. Thus, the series is also a bridge from the 1964 anthology to the present.

These four poets in the Oregon Literature Series know one another. And, generally, so do all the eight poets. In addition, some of the eight met for the first time in a workshop, and a number of these workshops were taught by one of the "Five Poets of the Pacific Northwest." This is not surprising given that all eight poets have been writing poetry for at least 20 years. Three Oregon magazines—*Calapooya Collage, Fireweed,* and *Hubbub*—have published five of the eight poets.

Of the "Five Poets of the Pacific Northwest," one was not a student of Roethke: William Stafford. Stafford came to the Northwest in 1948, as did Bernard Malamud and Leslie Fiedler. Of the three, only Stafford stayed. He made Oregon his home. Oregonians saw Stafford as one of their own and were proud. Over the years he became an Oregon tradition, with an uncanny knack for making poetry legitimate to the general public, a benefit Northwest poetry and poets still enjoy.

Certainly, the eight poets of this anthology benefitted from Stafford's presence. Many of them knew him; some took workshops from him. They heard him read his poems. Primarily through Stafford, I believe, did these eight Oregon poets draw from the contribution of the *Five Poets of the Pacific Northwest*. There is a poetry prize in Oregon in William Stafford's honor, and its first winner was Susan Spady, one of the eight poets in this anthology.

We three editors enjoy the sense of working in a community of

Northwest poetry anthology editors dating back to *Five Poets of the Pacific Northwest*. Until this particular anthology appears, we editors are the only people, as far as we know, who know the work of all eight Oregon poets. So we await publication eagerly. May the book create new readers for these poets.

Peter Sears
June, 1999
Corvallis, Oregon

Millennial Spring

Susan Spady

Among Susan Spady's earliest memories are "prickly gorse and harsh winds, crashing storms, mineral smells, sand warming and sticking to my feet, pearly linings of mussel shells, barnacles sharp underfoot, and agates blinking from wet sand" —impressions from her childhood years in Bandon, Oregon, which prompted her to begin writing. Spady graduated from Lewis & Clark College in 1969, then left Oregon to live for two years in Chicago and seven in Alaska. She has since been variously rooted in Western Oregon, where she earned her M.F.A. at the University of Oregon in 1986. Presently, she makes her home in Corvallis with her eleven-year-old daughter; two grown children are on their own. She has supported herself through freelance editing, and recently began a cottage industry making computer wrist rest pillows. Organic gardening and Breema bodywork are two of her primary interests. "During much of my life I've been searching for a way through illness, and Breema, along with writing, has become an essential part of my quest for healing." For inspiration and support she thanks her writing colleagues, in Portland some years ago and now in the Willamette Valley, especially Donna Henderson and Sandy Diamond. In 1993, Spady was chosen Oregon's first William Stafford Poet.

Carrying Eggs

If you're sure you won't spill them,
Grandma said, and I held my breath
from the hen house to her kitchen,
afraid the still warm eggs would hatch
in mid-air. They were the-world-on-my-
shoulders my father always told me
I couldn't carry. Shaky, I set them down.

Years later, I walked past protesters wearing
black arm bands, and hugged
books to my chest. My arms ached
for their weighty signs. When I raised my hand
in class I could hardly speak.

Now I have this girl-
child with her swagger and trumpet
voice. She's barely a year
as a hundred thousand eggs form
in her miniature baskets.
She will march, shout, make waves,
and they won't spill. She is their reckless
keeper, and they, spirals of song
drifting the fragile
earth's breath.

Underpants

        showed when girls climbed the monkey
bars so some girls didn't. Some who did
would kick a boy in the mouth if he got smart.
Others showed off their pink and lace,

wiggled high overhead as boys yelled
London, France. Earthbound, I sucked in
my pot belly and tried to stand in some regal way
so a book on my head, when I walked,

wouldn't fall—Daddy said. Mine
were never panties, were plain
as oxfords correcting my feet. By junior high

those fancy-pants climbers were cheerleaders
flirting from under their minis, tossing
smiles at the crowd through pearled lips.
They did splits: hello,

from between our legs! And my book
slid off frontways now, sweaters revealing
empty puckers, bras I made only a dent in
and slouched to hide. I didn't think much

about underpants. I was sealed shut,
spoke sarcastic nothings to boys, prayed
every night for God to make me
sinless and new. While pompoms exploded

like fireworks from cheerleaders' fingers, I sat
in the bleachers distorting my face
on my saxophone, wearing the Pep Band's sickly
gold, my disdain for those high-kickers—

but it's all right. Because first
I stopped going to Sunday School
and then wearing underpants—opened my stride
to winds that long full skirts

gathered in. I visited London and France,
climbed stairways with risers of blue sky
over men always looking
but never upward.

The Wishing Pool

The two of you, grown lunky
as tennis shoes in a dryer, grip with your
toes and stretch. Your hands stalk coins,
make bridges of your bodies. With arms
like wipers clearing drizzle, you embezzle

wishes. I warn
of hypothermia, it's March,
your sweatshirts soaked.
Too late for warnings, anyway: your wills,
grown huge, unmotherable, sweep me
aside.

       Yet when I'm wheeled from anesthesia,
sutures in my womb, your voices float
joyous down my torpid blood.
You hold my hands and feed me chips of ice
that glitter like doubloons.

Child of Somalia

               multiplied
by a million daily
newspapers, I can't imagine
your head on its thin stalk
like the aliens children draw;
your hair crumbled, oddly red;
your dried skin, stuck
to spongy bone—could it possibly
soften and expand, if you were to
eat, to eat and eat, until the food
satisfied the world of hunger
until your body, if it remembered how,
could make something beyond protracted death.

I can't imagine how your arms might feel,
wintered cornstalks, your flesh
of old gourds. Your mother
without a drop to wet your lips,
without a spoon of gruel to urge your way,
without flesh of her own to comfort you.
Your mother collapsing on the way home,
spilling everything, your body scattered
on the desert, dry twigs; and you
gathering one foot, the other, pushing forward,
your blood scraping dry river beds; your heart
stumbling between beats.

Practice This Ending

When I took my children fishing
you refused to go. *Too dangerous*—
your guitarist's nails filed
to perfection. No one got hurt.
But my line snagged, whispered out
to vanishing. Helpless to stop it, I watched

you drift back east, guitars with slackened
strings in their velvet-lined, waterproof
cases. By now you've taken them out
to retune, filaments pulled from my flesh—

the Scarlatti, early in love,
your nails edges of moon
in the dim room. Snow
slid from the roof—fish belly
quick at the window.

The Scarlatti, my birthday
party, the bright A major
when I didn't like how you said
This is for Susan, making me feel
a spectacle of wanting
your love for my children.

So now, the piano blurred,
I practice this ending. The same sonata,
these last lines where I lean
the appoggiatura to A
and rest it there.

The Last Day

On my bike I dodged the bird,
already dead. Not large
or small not yet come
into blue or into its sure instincts. Smacked
by human speed.

                      The second day I winced,
not wanting to be reminded, its gray color
sodden, sunk inward. The third, I thought
I'd move it off the shoulder—
but pedaling uphill into wind—

it wasn't stopping that seemed impossible,
but to start again. The fourth, I thought
my pity was exhausted; the fifth,
its feathers lifted
as the body shrunk.

                      On the next day, yes,
it seemed to want to fly, more of air than
earth, it asked
for nothing. On the last day, the seventh,
I began the poem, the bird
flying behind me, its beak in the base

of my brain, its wings thrashing
as if to fly into the tree
that groans in the skull. And I worked hard
against the wind, listening

for the poem—but not at once—for first
I went home, sliced thick bread
and ladled soup—and I glanced

at the newspaper on the seventh day,
at the photograph of children, their heads
wobbling like lost planets, their being sucked
dry to leave only
the gaze, that longing for ferocious
joy, that longing which no longer
remembers what it longs for

                and on the last
day the poem stirs and the child opens
her mouth to ask, is there more?

Bruised

The woman who says we are spiritual
beings learning to be human, who says
she never wanted to be here,
in a body, orders
a smoked eggplant sandwich.
Her earrings whisper dusky-hued
niobium, her teal jacket
shimmers.

A purple cabbage leaf
lies by the public library,
on the sidewalk near the people
huddled in rain. They beg
listlessly; in this weather,
no one stops. The leaf, stepped on
many times, grows page on page
with texture. It reads itself
into my hunched walk, a strange dulse
glow as if undersea, a ship of ribs
and satin. A fibrous outer leaf
bleeding where bruised.
There is no ordinary life.

Grief

Who would have guessed that this
is grief—this sinking into the dark
texture of sacher torte, parceling
anxious oblivion over my tongue.
Because my mother once raised
a wire coat hanger over my face,
because my father's rage
turned me to a blue glint,
a vanishing beetle. I've worshiped

grief among the emotions, as if
it is better to pick stones
from the garden beds, spring after
spring, not understanding
how each winter pushes more up,
and it becomes too late to plant.
Greedy with grief, I pile
the stones, claim them
as my own—bulbs of iris tumored
behind my ribs, symphonies grating
in hip sockets.

                Perhaps if I only watched—
the newborn light of seedlings,
the shine of rain on stones—
grief would break into song
and my mouth would know to make
its own sweet taste.

Pretending

> *Let's pretend this is the toothbrush*
> *that the egg carton loves so much.*
> —Emily (age 2)

And so it is in that other world—
things love each other, even
things that are standing in
for other things, for every-
thing stands for love, for some-
thing beyond itself which shines
through it. And so we must ask
what it is we stand for, what shines
in us, through us, and if no-
thing, then why, and what
have we forgotten; ask how
we could forget the light in every
cell and atom, forget this world,
this dance of light and love—
forget that by pre-
tending, we make it so?

Flower Leaning from a Vase

One of her breasts
is small and lovely, the other
gone. She practices
asymmetry, flower
leaning from a vase,
rock at the edge
of a bare sill.
She marvels that once
she thought them puny.
Looks with one eye, outward,
inward: does a man
with no legs
have a spirit
sliced off like bread?
And does it grow back?
What of a starving child
whose bones are chalky shadows?

She watches a woman walk home
from church, wig set just so,
Bible clutched to her blank
chest. What does the body house,
except a dream of perfection?
And what houses the body?
When she filled her babies' bottles
she forced a river
back into small dry fists.
The doctor advised it.
She traces the mound of fruit
not picked, and then, her tender
scar. Could a man stroke this?
And find her?

Victoria Wyttenberg

Victoria Wyttenberg grew up in Grants Pass, Oregon. "My obsessions go back to my growing up there, often in family issues, and in feeling a solace from the natural landscape, the Rogue and Applegate Rivers, the hot summer sun and the smell of rain." Wyttenberg went on to University of Oregon, Oregon State University, and Southern Oregon College, where she completed a Masters Degree in Humanities. In 1974, she and her present husband "tried to do the difficult, if not impossible task of putting our two families together." For thirty years, she has taught high school English, mostly in Beaverton, where she lives. Her first experience in poetry took place in 1977: a workshop at Haystack in Cannon Beach with poet Richard Hugo. Wyttenberg likes to quote Hugo: "The poem is always in your hometown, but you have a better chance of finding it in another." The following year, Wyttenberg joined Carolyn Miller, another poet of this anthology, in a Haystack workshop with Sandra McPherson. She and Miller have remained friends since. Wyttenberg earned a M.F.A. in poetry at the University of Washington in 1989, and for her poems she has won two prizes: the Richard Hugo Prize from Poetry Northwest in 1980 and the Academy of American Poets at the University of Washington in 1990.

Curve and Connection

For a month my right foot has been wrapped
like a mummy, toes lined up, bruised
fat sausages. My left foot is tired
from hopping. A doctor cut bones and held them
with metal. It will be a strong foot, he said.

Not a lotus foot, not delicate like the doe's hoof,
not the foot of a woodpecker holding to tree trunks,
or the sticky foot of a fly clinging to the ceiling,
not tough as the crab or good for eating,
more like a jellyfish slapping along through surf,

a foot that knows healing with scars to prove it,
a foot for walking down Broadway or the Champs Élysées.
The heel comes down hard. Remember Achilles.
Aching, veiny, phalanges, metatarsals, tendons, wrinkled
brave, willing to take my weight for this journey toward dust.

Foot in my mouth, rough as a potato, addicted
to leather, a monument to hinges and the humble
fat padded and calloused sole, a miracle
of balance, curve and connection in spite of bunions,
corns, ingrown toenails, odors bad as a barnyard,

feet worthy of red shoes and washings in rose water.
We set out full of hunger, bridge of the arch
curved for a kiss. The dead push up
from the underworld through twigs and dry grass
into the soles of my feet, and here I am.

Flowers Have Beauty and Roots Have Worth

Father sends me out to fetch you
but nothing makes you want to come.
Coatless and barefoot, you sit in the field

more reliable than love.
Queen Anne's Lace and Blue Sailors,
stems filled with milky juice

never molesting anyone, brush your arm.
I remember you thin, when you and father danced
so close no one could cut in.

"Mother, come home." I plead.
"I'd love to, but I can't," you say.
You tell me the story

of James James Morrison's mother
who drove to the end of town in her golden gown
and never returned, the story of three foxes

who didn't wear stockings and kept their handkerchiefs
in cardboard boxes. I don't quite know where
we are going, toward yarrow, beautiful

and worthless, clover, evening primrose.
We could try to explain father's seed
you opened wide for, that made me bloom

beside you in this field.
Blow a dandelion at its weediest.
The moon opens its mouth,

lets out a light like father's flashlight.
Stones crown through the earth. Here we are,
slumped over like cabbages.

Silver Milkweed tricks the insects
until a whole podful of babies
drifts off. Who knows what will happen

when a man takes a woman's hand,
when she touches his face, when her body
bends to his slapping?

The School Photographer

The photographer had a room like a box where he controlled
the light, kept prints all shades of grey
like father's hair. In the morning he could make twilight,
in mid-day, midnight, shuttering stars,
reflectors, metal moons. He knew how to airbrush scars.

His wife sat under a blanket
in a wheelchair he pushed to football games,
wheels spindled silver.
I pictured lovemaking, saw him lift her
gently into bed where she lay calm, nude, immobile.

Did her soul glow
in the dark like an alarm clock?
My father walked past me to get to mother.
Once she locked the door and he broke it
to splinters. One night he pushed her downstairs.

Maybe he wanted her wheelchair - bound
but she lay in a heap, cried, then walked away.
One morning the photographer called me from class
for yearbook pictures. He said light following
his hand would be lovely on my hair.

I thought of my body passing through the lens
like a ghost, becoming one-dimensional,
kept forever on paper in the pose he shaped.
Then he asked me to lift my pleated skirt
from my saddle shoes so he could see
the angle of my legs.

Higher, he said, lift it higher
as he arranged the shadow.
He wasn't handsome and I didn't like him
but thought of his wife in her wheelchair,
of father when he broke down the door
and I stood, letting him change the light.

Imprecation Against Adultery

You found a woman who liked your eyes
and led her right to bed.
For seven years I have imagined her
in every shape:
a black dress moving to music,
a long wet head of hair,
a rush of evening odor,
blonde spread-eagle.

Before my eyes the fork is the dance
you danced with her,
the spoon is your spine.
Her face is a fly in my soup.

The owl sings and the cat wonders
what to do for a ring.
A hard shadow hovers over us all.
My thoughts rise with your breath.

In that hotel room, your shirt a white flag
thrown over the back of a chair,
her hair tangled as widow's weeds.
May your mouth freeze
at the ice-cold thought of me.

House for Sale

Dandelion in the lawn. Bicycle tires
out of the garage, sheets over ivy. A man
comes back from the dead and continues
a fight with his son.

The boy drops the cat out the window.
The dog barks on and on,
sixty years, waking a woman
who wrings her hands into mothwings.

The woman returns as a child
to play hopscotch, and always
arrives home first, and jump rope:

> Gypsy gypsy please tell me
> What my husband's name will be.

In the kitchen she helps herself
then throws her doll into the kettle.
Its rag head floats on a slice of potato.
Somewhere a horse blows to wake the water.

New owners can't find a seat at the table or a bed
to sleep in. They hang garlic over the door
and take mustard to make a cross on the wall
but spirits chant back:

> This house has four corners
> and spirits adore it.

Bird Shadows

The owl is still staring into the night,
looking for something, crying
through her heart-shaped face.
One screech warns of death,
three of marriage.

An owl's hoot sounds cold
on a winter's night,
absorbed by clouds and dew,
then quiet as if the owl were never there.

The robin knows what fell last year,
the apples' hope.
Swallows sing from branches
of the plum tree.
Ravens do not return.

In a dream I bathe in a puddle,
hands becoming wings,
and I can never look back
for a lost mate or a child I can recognize.

What's an arm?
The past is lost like far off earth.
What does sky mean?
Heaven everyday.

The Curse

The style in those days was saddle shoes,
marry young and follow his blue smoke:
now you may hit the bride.

I wish you a long life with your mother.
Be bald, both of you, and may your eyes
cloud over. She will live forever, forever beat

on the bathroom door. Stammer through breakfast.
Chew slowly, remembering something.
Repeat old stories in each other's hairy ears.

May she be the only woman you hear moaning.
Get up from sleep each night and never find
what is missing. You'll live but you won't feel like loving.

Even hairs get in the way of your weakness.
You fall to the floor but no one notices.
You look just like the linoleum.

Whack pears for light.
You are the frog that never changes.
Someone has your legs for supper.

Memory will not go to sleep
and you must bury your father over and over
to keep from dreaming.

You wake up an old man, the past circling
above your head in smoke from your cigarette.
Your mother is still watching.

Each night you wet the bed. Everyone
in the neighborhood looks in the windows, laughing.
Your dog goes off and you jump straight up

on the end of his chain all day, waiting.
He never returns. The moon slips away.
Crows peck at your eyes, cawing.

The children know names of wildflowers
but forget yours. The warmest thing you stroke
is your gun. Your shoes can't run.

Blueberries

These blueberries are for you, Zoe,
for your breakfast. On the farm
when I was a boy, I picked berries
every summer, only the ripe ones,
cleaned the bush. A farmer could always
come along and say, not fast enough
or clean enough, and fire you. Now,
when my fingers touch the berries, they know
just what to do, the right touch, not too rough,
just full ripe berries, deepest blue. But it isn't color
tells me ripeness as much as touch.
Berries come right off in my hand. Picking's easy.
Milking too. My fingers know.
If I touched a cow's udder right now
I'd know just how to pull. I had a calf once
I really loved. I still remember that day
I came home from school. I was about six,
Zoe, younger than you, and I walked into the barn
when my father was slaughtering my calf,
the calf I loved. Nobody punished me for crying
but nobody talked about it either, and nobody
warned me. I didn't cry when my daughter
was killed in her car. My wife and I went to California
for the funeral, and that damn yellow Volkswagen
was parked by the garage and her husband, Larry,
said he was keeping it for parts. I couldn't say
anything. On the way back on the plane
my wife said, "Don't ever touch me again."
My daughter had just had a baby.
She was killed in January, ground so cold
we couldn't even bury her.

Blue Heron

She is the blue distance
of everything we kiss,
the guttural cry of departure.
How can any of us protect ourselves?
My husband turns from me
and the dead slip in.
The heron is bent
like an old woman.
She is a solitary feeder
and I am afraid
my very presence drives her away,
but I return often
when she isn't there,
watching changes of light
on water. I look for blue
on the edge, the promise
of plumage. Between dusk
and darkness the moon rises
and the heron appears,
still as wood pilings.
She knows how to avoid
storms and how to be alone,
staying in shallow margins,
waiting. Cold air wraps
the landscape. My body is turning blue.

For My Oldest Child

*"I saw the angel in the marble
and I just chiseled till I set him free."
Michelangelo*

To be a child again she will go back
past her own grey house, the yard with trees
the table, oak chairs, the toaster,

past the child born before the wedding dress.
She will have to go past shoes used as weapons
to saltwater sandals and rubber boots

that know their way through the woods,
past the white island of hospital bed
where she moaned, "The roses are lovely,

but angels have ruined my cake."
The maple drops red leaves in a language
only for children.

The moon is a ripe banana.
She gives up the leather jacket
for the blue snowsuit with a hood,

its mittens safe on strings.
The fence is for pictures.
Gates, doors, windows, let a child out,

let her in.
A rag doll clearly has a heart,
but to get there she must get past glass

her father broke with his fist,
the belt he used for beating.
To find that holy child,

she must put her heart in her pocket
and carry it like a woolly treasure
past the black sun to the crayoned yellow one

drawn over a house with a path
and a brown cow.
A wolf is the dog who licks her face.

Every garden has secrets.
Sunflowers bend their heads to a child
and corn gives silk.

Charles Goodrich

Charles Goodrich is a poet and essayist, a professional gardener, and a literary and environmental activist. About his own poetry, Goodrich says, "I want my blue-collar friends and neighbors to have full access to my work. I hope my poems achieve a level of vividness and subtle music that pleases the connoisseur as well, but never at the cost of clarity and meaning." Strongly influenced by classical Chinese and Japanese and contemporary Eastern European poetry, Goodrich says, "I probably read more poetry in translation than poetry written in English." Goodrich grew up in small towns in Ohio and Illinois. After college, hitch-hiking south from a summer job in Denali National Park, he arrived in Portland "as flute music drifted through the city on the very day that Tom McCall Riverfront Park opened with an uproarious celebration. On the spot I became an Oregonian." Goodrich tends the grounds of the Benton County Courthouse and he and his wife built their home and "garden strenuously on a flatland acre at the rural edge of Corvallis." They are active in environmental and land use issues. Recently, he organized a reading and edited a chapbook in honor of the Willamette River, which rolls through town. A founding member and past president of the Willamette Literary Guild, Goodrich was a 1996 Fishtrap Fellow and the winner of a 1998 literature fellowship from the Oregon Arts Commission.

Millennial Spring

The factory squats at the confluence of the rivers, where the Kalapuya had a potlatch ground. In vacant lots nearby, purple camas is blooming. Turkey vultures roost in cottonwood groves by the river. Beavers and foxes on nighttime errands ignore each other. There's a park with soccer fields and hiking trails, a littered encampment where bleary men roll up in blue tarps, and a skinny-dipping beach on the gravel bar.

My house is up the street, beyond the cemetery. Last night when I rode my bike past the factory I stopped and wrote –

> Night shift whoosh
> of steam. A forklift's
> back-up beeper.
> The factory wheezing
> wounded air.

The factory wants to expand. I find myself along with dozens of neighbors organizing in opposition. The factory makes fiberglass. The air we breathe is studded with microscopic shreds of glass. After another late night meeting, six of us lean on our bicycles, talking. This is our social life, of late: strategy meetings and streetcorner hand-wringings. All of us are tired and grumpy. Suddenly I smell something.

> Shut up!   Smell that
> cottonwood sap?
> We've missed
> the arrival of spring.

I work as the gardener for the County Courthouse, and I'm way behind. Today I pruned the roses, the latest I have ever done so. As always, an elderly lady regards my severely pruned canes and asks, "Young man, do you know what you're doing?" Riding home in the evening I see a man at the back door of the factory, smoking a cigarette and gazing at the sky.

> Yes, the gibbous moon
> is lovely
> through safety goggles.

The comet, Hyakutake, has been visiting the past few nights, a swatch of stardust in the eastern sky. After our son is asleep, my wife and I go out into the garden and hold each other and gaze at it.

      Warm shoulders, fragrant hair.
      When this comet comes again

      we'll be gone.

The next night the comet has moved a little north, and the exhaust plumes from the factory rise toward it.

      Your presence, comet,
          sweetens somehow the evening's
              aroma of skunk.

We have done a prodigious amount of research, read medical journals, studied the arcane language of pollution-control engineering. We cannot get the men at the factory to acknowledge any shred of possibility that there may be adverse health effects from respiring glass fibers. This tends to exaggerate our fears.

      One must hope
      that the great blue heron
      fishing in the factory's settling pond
          catches nothing.

To sit in the backyard grass, to lean and loaf while my son plays trucks in his sandbox—it doesn't happen much lately. Today, however, the sun was narcotic. I could not pursue the chores I had planned.

      The plum tree in full blossom—
         slower than this
        time
      does not go.

After a quick snooze on the chaise lounge, though, I begin to hear the unmowed grass growing at my feet, and weeds overwhelming the herbs in the garden. All right, then, to work!

> Affliction of spring—
> blossoms
> I haven't time to admire.

Later in the afternoon:

> My son, fishing the dry ditch
> for pretend fish
> has drawn an audience
> of crows.

Five hundred people attend the hearing. One woman speaks of the fox she has seen trotting beside the river. A man tells how geese fly right over the factory's smokestacks. Several speakers dwell on the children who run up and down the soccer fields in the shadow of the factory, while others discuss the epidemiological studies and laboratory tests, the evidence of lung disease and cancer. A woman roundly pregnant invokes seven future generations.

Those few who talk in favor of the permit—all men, as it happens, most of them in suits and ties—speak in the cliché of factuality. "There is no reason to believe that these glass fiber emissions constitute any threat to the health of the community."

There is no reason to believe something huge isn't rolling over all of us.

On the way home, to calm myself, I stroll among the gravestones—

> The Big Dipper—
> what's it pouring
> into the smokestacks?

The month of April is cold and rainy. Blossoms are blown off the cherry trees as quickly as they open. I hole up in the boiler room in the basement of the Courthouse, drawing planting designs for the annual flower beds, writing letters to the editor. In the brief interludes of sunshine, I mow the Courthouse lawns, exulting.

> Ah, to travel in a land
> where everything is new and strange—
> my home town after rain.

On the first of May I plant pansies in the flower beds in front of the Courthouse. The soil is beginning to warm, my spade turns up fat earthworms. From the screen-roofed exercise-yard of the Gray Bar Hotel come shouts of some raucous ball game.

> Passersby stop and scowl
>   at the sound of laughter
>   coming from the jail.

The permit is granted. The factory begins to expand, growl a little louder. The air is lacerated. There are billions of glass fibers in it. I'm not leaving. Ever.

> The red-shafted flicker
> calls that old maple home.
> But for courting
> he prefers to drum
> on sheetmetal gutters.

The Insects of South Corvallis

1) Two Mosquitoes in the Bathtub

They've been here for weeks
living on leaky faucet drips.
When I draw a bath, they fly a little
but soon settle back among the soap stains.

It's December, freezing outside.
That's why they don't bite me, or mate.
Enormous desires encoded on their chromosomes
lie dormant. They dream of summer.

Relaxing in hot water, I watch them
doing nothing. One, the male,
waves his feathery antennae. He's smaller
and has a broken foot. The female
is slightly swayback,
maybe just tired. Science
and Buddhism I call them,
orphan twins in search of lost family,
a couple of itinerant trapeze artists,
a secretly amorous pair of saints.

Whoever they are, they're my guests.
We're sharing our morsel of eternity.
We bathe together.

2) Sowbugs

Vagabonds, hobos, they trundle in
through a crack in the wall by the back door
and congregate under the washing machine
to drink soapy drainwater.

I'm not running a bug hotel. My home
is no flophouse for backyard dropouts.
But these folks are easy company.
They aren't evangelists
reveling all night in confessional raptures
or teenage sons of bankers
cranking stereos and snorting coke.
They aren't revolutionaries or reactionaries,
atheists, pagans or co-dependents.

They're just little bugs
who've seen the world some
and like to swap stories around the floor drain.

3) Yellowjackets

Cold as mummies
they come inside with the firewood
where an hour beside the stove revives them,
resurrects them
to their ancient throne
of pure animosity.

They throb. They buzz.
Suddenly they blaze against windows,
whack lampshades, attack the light.

I understand. I suspect
that I, too, am of royal parentage
and I awaken sometimes
enraged at having been so cruelly deposed
from the heights of power and grace.

4) *Silverfish*

These shy bristletails
    are quick
        as calligraphy.

Squashed
    they make a vague Chinese
        ink wash across the paper.

I know I seem
    inscrutable to them:
        an American

blue-collar male, married
    but solitary
        scratching poems in the night

while they busy themselves
    being law-abiding insects
        metamorphosing nymph to adult

without complaining
    even though
        it's a hell of a headache.

The millions of eggs
    they lay in my walls
        I can forgive.

What I hate is—
    (maybe somebody's
        got to do it

but if fills me with loathing)
    —they eat
        books.

5) Ladybugs

Every January they re-emerge,
anchorites from within our walls,
and cloister themselves on the upstairs window
for a few weeks of fasting and travail.

By day they wander the glass
like desert mendicants, each bug
nothing but a robe and a begging bowl.

By night they huddle
in a corner of the casement,
a little heap of rosary beads,
a handful of prayers incarnate.

Winter being the season of doom,
I have my own austerities to attend to.
But, mornings, when I find
their eclipsed bodies on the windowsill,
lovely and empty as little lacquered urns,

I sweep them up with a feather duster
and return them to the garden.

6) *Fruitfly*

That miserable winter I drank so much
there was this fruitfly
who loved to land on my lips.

I called her Mabel
(not her real name)
and told her my life's story,
all the women I'd done wrong,
the generally rotten guy I'd been.

Not a smidgen of sympathy.
All she wanted
was to dance.
If I started talking
she'd tickle my moustache.
If I blew her away
she'd flirt right back again.

Pity wasn't in her bag of tricks.
She loved me, she whispered once,
simply for the sweetness of my breath.

Heavenly Bodies

Aglow with fever,
my infant son twitches asleep
as I rock him in my lap afraid to stop.

Outside the window the airport searchlight
wipes the gingko in the dark backyard.
Higher up, against the constellations,
American astronauts are dissecting rats.
I'm utterly weightless
in the orbit of my cried-out child.

Blinking lights are jetliners.
Wavery ones are satellites.
My baby whimpers. A small plane whines.
Nightmares, like flights above an airport,
circle us, waiting to land.

Now he sleeps. Now he wakes.
Sleeps. Wakes. Cries. Screams!
His first tooth is a rocket in his flesh.
The searchlight turns and turns on its stump.

He wakes again, and finally stares
from deep quiet into deep space.
Look there, measly one, flying in the south—
that's Pegasus, the winged horse,
born from Medusa's severed neck.

And there's Andromeda, the Chained Lady—
that broach of stars on her breast
is the farthest light a father can see
with his naked eye.

Hover Fly

at Fishtrap

The Methodist Camp at Wallowa Lake
is a Game Refuge—the deer
stroll through morning and night,
chipmunks take pumpkin seeds right from your hand,
and the Steller's Jays are even picking up syllables
of our language.

Watching a four-point buck
grazing beside the basketball court,
I feel an urge to leap out of my chair
and yell, "BANG!"

or, perhaps better, to go stand in the center of the lawn,
palms upraised,
and blither some sort of anti-
Franciscan sermon, a quiet
and bloody synopsis of American history
to inoculate these innocents
with a dark dose of late 20th century cynicism, "Friends,
    do not be deceived. This is not
    the Peaceable Kingdom. Only
    a tiny incongruous island
    in the ocean of brutality . . ."

But, just then, a hover fly
lands on my arm. Six bristly feet
brush through the hairs on my wrist
and now she's sipping sweat
from the back of my hand—it tickles!
I try to hold still. I want to ask her,
    "Do you think we can do it—just be
    a refuge, with bugs and people
    and foxes and grasses and whole seasons passing
        through,
    eating and being eaten,

>   abiding in a quiet
>   and desperate
>   equilibrium
>   forever?"

Stinging Nettles

Murky water in the slough,
the oily sheen and bitter smell
of herbicides and sewage. That deeper stink
is the natural putridity of drowned fescue
decaying anaerobically, and it rouses me
like a whiff of sulphur from hell.
I'm here for nettles, for a spring
slumgullion of bitter herbs, and the edges
of swampy ex-river bottoms
are where to go with gloves on and rose snips.

The osoberry bushes
are leafing out beside heaps
of broken concrete. Shattered green
wine bottles wink among wild blue violets.
Winter's gunshot possum has vanished, but now
here's a rufous-sided towhee just back from Mexico.

Cottonwood pollen floats in long swirls
on the slack water. I sit on the muddy bank, cursing
and smiling. They say nettles
are richer in vitamins than spinach. I'm not
Popeye. I steam them for a homeopathic dose
of poison. I may be chronically pissed off, but
I'm a singer of praises, to the end,
and I need those needles
lining my throat.

Barbara Davis

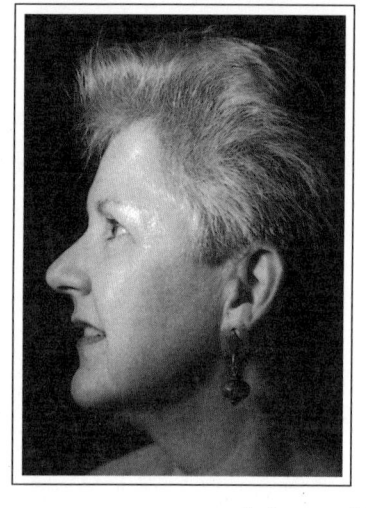

Born in The Dalles, Barbara Davis grew up on a ranch in eastern Oregon, near Condon, went on to high school in Salem and, at Willamette University, studied piano and music theory. Niece of Oregon writer H. L. Davis, Barbara next took up theatre and then, in San Francisco, with friend and poet Ina Cumpiano, explored writing poetry. Cousin Martha Gatchell, also a poet, convinced her to take a summer poetry workshop at Menucha, high above the Columbia River Gorge, sponsored by the Creative Arts Community. Returning to Menucha for a series of summers, Davis wrote many poems and met poets with whom she has remained friends for years, two of whom are Barbara Conyne and Pat Ware. Ware's work is in this anthology. Davis then moved back to Oregon, settling in Southeast Portland. She joined the Portland Poetry Festival Board, became its president, and went on to diversify its activities. In 1997, Davis left a two-year position as executive director of Northwest Print Council to return to her long-time career as a law firm administrator in Portland. Two of her favorite books of poems are Louis Glück's *Arrarat* and C.K. Williams' *Tar*. About her own work she says, "I believe in the inherent energy of all things, that they are all of one piece. That's the connection I keep trying to make."

Come Together Down the Canyon Where It Was Good

This time your grandfather sits in the front porch shade,
    watching the hill and the spring where the deer drank
    when he lived here

This time, your father's brother is younger, on horseback,
    out of sight of the rest of the family—
    you don't see his face but you know it
    from his stories

This time in her doorway, your grandmother: white-dress pale,
    as if she is her just-married photograph, then
    she changes, bride to grandmother to bride, and keeps looking
    to you as if you are the cause

This time your aunt comes towards you saying she will stay
    and it is not wartime

This time your uncle ties his horse to the front gate
    so he can sit next to his father, and a speckled dog
    who comes unbidden to lie down in the dead grass

This time just in front of the granary a one-legged man rests
    his cane on a Persian carpet and remembers
    how it all was with his sons

And this time his wife comes quietly clear,
    her slim body shadows the oil lamp she turns down
    so this time you can see

the generations of mothers and fathers, returned
    and preparing to leave, but still able to look back
    on the dust, on what was, and on their child
    so unable to rest.

Conversation in the Dark

> *Because they do not chirp, female crickets are not kept by the Chinese. They are fed to birds.*
> —sign in the Leland Stanford Jr. Museum

My mother opens boxes of silks
her mother never wore,
piles tissue between us.

I might crawl under my brass bed
and not touch my back.

If the closet door opened,
my grandmother would come out.
In the mirror, I have a silvery shadow.

The bed moves when you are not looking.
I am surrounded by antlers.

They offer hats to someone very tall.
The deer look back from very far away.

Outside, cheat grass scratches in the roses.
The closet by the bed makes other sounds.

My uncle says the Chinese keep things in cages,
but I can't remember seeing one.

There are always people in another room
saying things you can't hear.
Except your name, you hear.

Tomorrow my mother will go
into the closet. To clean, she says.

My uncle shows me a little box,
ivory and match sticks. He says
it is for crickets who won't sing.

The Artist at Fifty-One

for Keith Jones

Before he opened the box that I imagined having
a lid made of pearwood and apple, he began
to talk of his father. *I have this box
of my father's things that I keep in my room* . . .
Then he created it for me, suspending it
in moonlight, with his thick and practiced fingers
smoothing the familiar sides and top, easing the surface
with the memory in his hands, a shining,
until there in the night air and shadow
his fingertips slipped the delicate latch.
I keep what I have of his things there, he said,
opening the rounded cover with his forefinger.
Then touching one cufflink, rolling it aside,
he chose something his father had worn
to hold out to me. Perhaps it was a ring
because I could see between his finger and thumb
something suspended in the air. *Sometimes
I take them all out. I touch them. And hold them a while.*
And his fingers continued passing through the moonlight
and the air, now and again holding up something,
some thing he could hold, then put back.

Why the One-eyed Yellow Dog

Dying is no good for anybody,
but running a farm a woman gets used to it.

In ten years I buried a husband, what stock we had,
and lost the big elm out in front to the blight.

I stayed on for the quiet, sat on the stump
and watched sunsets come like your breath.

You almost wish you had a dog at sundown.

This one hung around till I promised I'd shoot him
if he came in the yard. Two days he laid out by the gate.

When I called him, he wouldn't come.
I took him water.

Why a one-eyed yellow dog picked me I don't know.
He stays out on the porch, eats my scraps. Won't come in.

One Syllable Villanelle

"I can't do spit!"
So what's not to do?
Wake up, get on with it!

When you want to quit
'cause you can't make blue
and you can't do spit,

make a game of it.
Try clay for the day.
Wake up! Get on with it.

Paste a smile on. It
won't hurt you. See?
"I can't do spit,"

you say? Not a whit!
Be the first one to
wake up. Get with it,

grump. Buck up and get
what you want! Don't stay
in one place with "can't do spit."
Wake up! Okay? Then get on with it.

The Bloom of Gold Needles

Needle One, placed in that soft curve
at the back of the neck where you were kissed
once, where the kiss itself lingers:
Brown birds jump and flit in a wild apple tree,
in the hedgerow, then they back into the fog.

Needle Two, balancing the first, on the left.
The breath lingers in pulpy skin. In the rose-gold
in the poster on the wall: dermis, epidermis . . .
where the body is an ocean of currents in purple
and green. *A fog bank lifting head high, or more*
over the scrub fence in the distant field
by the hill. No one else on the road today.

Three, placed a finger-width from the spine,
at the waist, her left-hand holding the flesh
still. Still. Ping! The gold stick.
The apple tree is the only thing, the red fruit
hanging and fallen. Old teasel holds up the dead grass.

Four, Five, Six in the grey wool that is pain
that is the saddle of the back.
Nothing so flat as a table you lie on,
nothing so empty as a bed, or wide as
the field you remember. *It's cold enough*
the gravel sticks together underfoot.

She spreads a yellow blanket over your legs
as if it were sand, but it is blue from your memory.
The soft threads undo themselves
automatically:
              Static overhead and into the street:
open the front door and through the echoing,
the doors and doors emptying outside into trees of starlings,
their black bodies sitting in the air.

The air and the blanket gather in the currents of the room,
they become a nothing as blue as the narrow channel of the air,
until there are no more trees, until there is only the echo
of waking and the blue voices of hydrangeas.

Chamber Work for the Eighth Day

for Mercedes Sousa

It could be morning or evening. The melody becomes
a tree against a pale sky, a woman singing,
and her song is also the shape of a tree or
perhaps an island or the shape of an island
where the words lay together as low waves
one over the other. And the cello (or a man
walking) laces in and out of the water or music
and passes as if music passed into shadow. Listen,

and after, you will discover a lake of lost things
and serenity—the one coming out of the other—
a place to rest, beneath a sky you remember, the clouds
reshaping themselves as an echo of the voice
in the song, perhaps in the language of trees.

Hills the Glacier Left Us

Floating things,
they move out pale and cool and on
as if they were the promises of mountains
that failed to point the way for what comes after.

How long? I want to know before we leave
the city, the thing she cannot answer.
Later I will point to how we're different,
the moves that don't feel right.
The mountains between us in bed:
if she could say how long it takes,
if I could choose the right path after moonrise,
if I could see mountains in the distance.

The things between us only seem to change.
If we move, it's with excuses. Paint
for fences we will point out later.
How we change, or if.
For example, how we move in sleep
kept separate by our elbows.

Afterward I tell myself
these are the things I mean to master:
how the mountains in Ontario could wear away;
how mountains rise in some men's daughters, why
we point to one and not the other,
how things could change, and how they might
be if I had come later, after . . . if I moved
with the slightest touch. If I were moved
as I want to be. If I were a lake
born after iceflows carved themselves in bedrock

because all things—mountain, water
might rest there—the point of it
always being to move on
and to stay after.

Paper Nautilus

Doesn't the shell seem to beckon you,
leading you onward to a chamber?
Or a chamber? Is it part of a fish?

If it were a woman's knee,
would you admire those simple bones,
the femur fitting so nicely there,
and acknowledge its engineering
moving one way and not the others,
its strength and flexibility?
Would you know the woman by her skin
(the fold at the back of that knee), or
the comfort hidden in her thigh—
or, imagining the feel of her, would you muse
on whether she would move to you or away,
on how soft she is, her belly?

Rotate this shell in your hand
to examine its belly
and with the tip of one finger
stroke that delicate hip.
Linger a while and let
the idea of her curl into you.
Feel how she floats,
how she jetted the ocean, pushing it
there just under the wave.
Now let your palm become water:
caressing her, changed by her beating—
a whorl on the surface.

The Explanation of Acorns

These acorns came from Laura's.

That afternoon we found a grove of live-oak,
each one old and partly covering a creek
the light turned silver.

I picked these
thinking we might bring them back
once she was well.
                        Thinking
it's a kindness not to name
the emptiness to come between
her ribs and her palm . . .

thinking it should be enough
to be alive
                and how it was for me—

although to say those words seemed
as wrong as telling her
                        it's easy . . .

telling how the surgeon marks your skin,
how you move and lose your balance,
how, from habit, you stop too far from the table
        or door,

how you give your body space
it no longer needs.

I never said
how tender you remain, afraid
to touch yourself; I never spoke
of waking
                with no feeling there.

Or, long after, how it was
to swim or brush against a lover's hand.

It was only when we turned for home
we spoke, and then
we spoke of trust. And breasts.

The two we each are born with.

Persimmons

I want what comes after the ocher leaf falls, after
it drifts the smoked air in late-October.
Afternoons. The thin light. No taffeta shade.
Not the leaf. I want the tree to show
itself a lean gray thing hung with abandon
bearing its fruit like oriental lanterns,
                                                as it is
when my yard fills and blushes with persimmons.
I want the deep frost when those bitter globes
drop into my hands newborn,
to leave them on neighbor's front porches
waiting, in brown paper sacks, to ripen the winter.

In the Garden of the Women

There were days I lay braced with pillows,
comforted by water from the corners of my eyes,
gliding back and back as if following
the history of tears—melting in my hair
as if she who lives in my eyes
could reach out, her cool fingers smoothing the veins.

There is enough water in each of us to make the sea
and we do this over and over, washing ourselves.
Without speaking, the women of this garden share secrets—
rinsing one another, their necks arching.
Footprints are forever dying.
Moss expands the walls, the floor.

And in his rain barrel, a carp, too old to see,
fans himself in the late afternoon.

Light slants into the pool until all of us are silent,
darting, languid—and she arches out
water collecting around her there on the bank
in pools—hardly enough if we are all fishes.

In the shallows at the edge of deep water I plan.
Will she see I have given up diving, my beautiful tail?
I dream of my tangerine tail.

A pearly carp waits for the tip of her hand.
When she does not come, I work my mouth, hoping,
circling the light until, breaking that blue,
orbits of her fingers dip down. She gathers me—
her breath, a ripple on the water.

The Blue Angel Raphael Breaks His Silence to Explain

No one is completely what he wants to be
not even angels.
And accidents can happen on the road.

I tell you now, my name is Raphael.
I have no past at all, my memory lasts
for the blink of a message. I know
just this one thing:

We are closer, you and I, than you think,
closer than protozoa or grass,
closer than the droplets in a cloud.

Wingless, I am unable to fly
although you imagined it.
                      And, now that you fly, you know
there is nothing so special in getting there faster.

Sometimes I am confused by what is good
or better.
                I ask myself is it too much
telling you what we are,
                        what goes on in our houses,
what kind of houses we have, and our rooms
                also and the secrets we keep
in the night; is it worth it
knowing we are what we are?

If what I lack is a human heart, I will go out anyway
into the day to talk and eat.
                  If there is no place in my body
to fit a human heart, I will comfort myself.
                        For the heart is a mysterious thing.
mine perhaps was given away, or perhaps
it is what I hold and have not discovered.

Debra Brimacombe

Intending to become a teacher when she was younger, Debra Brimacombe became, instead, a broadcast engineer, first at KUPL, and later at KEX and KKRZ. For nine years she has been supporting test applications for Audio Precision, a test equipment manufacturer in Beaverton, Oregon. Born in Hood River, Brimacombe grew up across the Columbia River in White Salmon, Washington, and with the exception of one year in Chicago, has been in the Portland area ever since. She and her husband live in Scappoose, Oregon and are devoted campers. Her interest in poetry comes from her two grandmothers, both of whom read verse to her. "One was a storyteller, the other wrote her own poems on the blank pages of her Bible. They taught me how to entertain my imagination in a book. I love Shakespeare and Keats. My favorite contemporary poet is Charles Simic." Brimacombe has worked with the poet Lisa Steinman. As to her own work, Brimacombe says, "I write because I read poetry. My heroes and heroines are poets. . . . When I write, I discover little facts about myself that accumulate and become knowledge about the world. I'm one of those persons who like to stay in hotels because the drawers are empty and I can arrange small quantities of my belongings in new ways."

Breakfast Bites

My brother's baby hangs
like a refrigerator magnet
on its mother's arm and spits up.

Hummingbirds appear.
Rufous and Anna buzz
and pant—
some land
on the red railing
that circles their primrose restaurant.

Frogs croak.

Beyond, roan horses graze
and step off the distance of the fence,

while someone, camouflaged,
somewhere,
in another room
flickers off a screen,
zips another body bag,
and counts: one; one; one; one.
A spoon dropped, clatters.

I rinse the remaining milk
out of my cereal bowl
and lean it against a couple of mugs
on the top dishwasher rack.

Two fronts—one low,
off the Pacific, are not affecting
traffic, but the change
in barometric pressure could.

High Desert

This is the boast
riding the hawk's wings above canyon walls
and the crow's call,
not the pantomime
shadow

but the sheer dust
eager for the wind
and the lizard
asleep on a sunburnt log.

This is the sagebrush
and the juniper
like immoral icons
indifferent to complaints,

and the dawn
that flicks dew
at wincing stars
then saunters whisker-free into the dusk.

Spans

When the fir trees fell in the storm,
their roots exposed like big toes
that had worn through their muddy socks
we knew we would never live long enough,

that every year a red ring had turned
brown, another year had been put to rest

and all those years stacked now
like blankets folded on our shelves
will never comfort us enough
without those forever green boughs

sweeping the skies above our house,
translating the wind's grandiloquence.

Simply Taught

Mary taught me to imagine
what frogs might be,
to twirl in a calico skirt,
and lift myself over the fence,
then she went to sleep.

I didn't know that frogs
could hop so far,
that fences could be nothing
but barbed wire,
and Mary could be so tired.

Before They Can Hang Up

I will remove the cradles from the phones
my grandmothers used, the worn hooks they
said goodbye into. I will eat soft pretzels
in New York and walk through the sprinkles
that fall from prayers issued from city squares,
and I will listen for the saxophone wail
as well as the bucks that butt the juniper stump
when their velvet needs to be rubbed.

Debra's Oak Tree

Like Mother
you are what I know
and what I can't ask:
the sieve in the brine
and the beckon
dark, under a green skirt—
the moist hands.
You are the breast holding me here
and the coffin lined with satin sheets.
You bounce like a balloon on a stick
and flutter like promises.
Your branches twist
the cupboards of my thoughts
until their doors buckle
and make me wonder
would I be here
if I could, like the robin
that seems to hop
from branch to branch
until it reaches the top,
soar off.

Intersection

You followed a path
borrowed from a deer, aware,
between the nibbled limbs of firs,
and maples robed in swaying webs,
careful not to wake the brown spiders
hanging like autumn's gorged ornaments.

Packed soil accepted your feet
as you crossed
              the yellow line
reflecting the center of a paved street.

You were an absence
              of glare
in the knowledge of my headlights

an instant of knowing—

I turned my radio down,
and as quickly you were gone.

You wore the hide of that deer, tanned
and stitched, and balanced
gourds of water on tethers
draped around your neck.

I grabbed the seat belt harness
stretched across my chest.

You turned to look
              at me
as if I were a blue-eyed crow landing
in the top of a fir or an eagle
dropping a feather
through a shaft of sunlight
that might land
              as we crossed
at your feet.

When the Flag was Raised Over the Hugh Whitson Memorial Elementary School (Back When it Was Called White Salmon Elementary School)

With both feet flat on the ground,
one hand over our hearts,
(usually our right hand over our left heart
except for Nancy, and sometimes me,
when we couldn't remember
which was right)
we watched the flag
lurch up the metal pole
while Mike pulled and pulled
down on the rope.
Nancy sometimes moved her feet,
but I was solid.   My Dad
was in the war.
When the flag reached the top
we all looked up,
heads rolled back,
backs arched,
mouths opened.
Then we pledged.   We were allegiant.
Every voice went up.   And on windy days
the flag clapped.

Autumn's Eaten Apple

This is the other side
of your apple:
the vacuum pull
of your bite,
the vacant flesh
crisp and full like your eyes
when laughter grabs your skin and
like a child's grip
opens your lips. This is the scent
of diamond and ruby dews,
the brag of bees,
the brown bruise lace of cider,
the drops of juice that dangle
from your knuckles
and glisten in the dimple
of your chin, juice that swirls
like a drunken jack
when you chew.

Swallows

I swoop
over the pond
a wide loop

a high bank
my wings spread,
the tips of sabers,

sharp and slicing.
A fly
roams,

a rustic
above
the lust

and leap
of a frog.
I lunge

and scoop
it up

delicious.
Another swallow
darts past:

a flash.
Its white breast
a flutter

in ascent.
I luff
in the brush

of an offshore
breeze.
We swoon,

loop, and wink
as we eat.

Take, Hold

You're the knuckles wrapped around the last ear
of corn in the garden, its tassels tacky from the mists
that crept through the morning,

its husk still green and nursing. You're the fist
that pressed down and ripped the scroll

of kernels from the its pale stalk. You're the palm
brushed with the glistening milk that oozed up cool
like a spring in the harvest's fissure and you're

the fingers that nudged the cob away from the leap
and gurgle revels of boiling water confined in a kettle.

Alone

When the moon tips,
like a lustrous ladle
that dips into the night
and scoops stars,
gorging its dark cup
until it's round with all light

I suspect the flecks
locked in the glare
of my glass slippers,
as well as the worn toes,
and the polished skin
on the bottoms of my feet,
but tonight I swear

the colors that blinked
those star-filled nights

were my eyes,
caught,
conspiring
with another pair of eyes,
both of us dribbling
our sloppy wishes
across the black sky.

Harold Johnson

"American culture as reflected in politics, the arts, and athletics seem to be my chief preoccupation." On the page, Harold Johnson likes to downplay his role and narrate culturally strange and perplexing experiences. Sometimes the stimulus is an overlap of language. One poem, for instance, is set off by the names of the Dutch painter Jan Vermeer and the American baseball pitcher John Vandermeer. Born in Yakima, Washington, Johnson's poetry began, he believes, with his mother. "A religious woman, she was possibly a latent scat singer, going around the house singing nonsense syllables." Then there was enjoying and excelling at reciting verse for programs at the Full Gospel Pentecostal Church. In high school, baseball took over. At college, the discovery was modern fiction. Following a stint in the army, Johnson became an English teacher. During this time, he was inspired to write poetry by poet Sandra McPherson, "The biggest influence on my poetry attempts." Johnson is now retired from teaching and lives in Portland with his wife, a painter and teacher. He continues to be active in the visual arts, and painting appears frequently in his poems. He participates in a poetry writing group, has served on the board of the Friends of William Stafford, and is co-editor, with Sidney Thompson, of *Fireweed*.

Stealing the Shortstop's Shoes

getting cleats was always a problem
couldn't hang onto caddying money
long enough for the price of a pair
my brother the junior american legion star
always got the shoes   somewhere i found some
dried-out hand-me-downs   oversized
felt like they had pebbles inside

after a legion game
hanging around the locker room
of the town's pro team   i lifted
shortstop crane's narrow new spikes
jesus but they looked slick
too tight and hard to run fast in
but i wore them anyway
(a grown man with a foot smaller
than an eighth grader's)

my friend gordon inquired, where'd ya get
those shoes
and i   whaddayou wanna know for
gordon didn't play ball
those look like les crane's shoes
he said   a brick fell in my gut
you don't know what you're
talkin about i said
those are crane's shoes he said
jabbing his finger at my cramped feet

that's all he said and left the field
that's all i ever heard about the crime

who was it that didn't do me the favor of arraignment
who told fatherless gordon to charge me

The Names of Summer: A War Memory
(an excerpt)

Early in the war they began to show up on Sundays
at the Washington Junior High School diamond—
the first baseball players I'd seen in uniforms,
twenty or so, wearing white uniforms with red
caps and stockings. At first, they all looked alike,
like a handful of toy soldiers, and their uniforms
seemed like a big white lily that tore into particles
as they piled out of the army truck that brought them
to the field. "Japs," a watching neighbor growled.
Their driver relaxed behind the wheel in his khakis
during games, flipping through magazines and puffing Camels.
He counted heads when they reloaded.

I hung out near the benches to drink in the hitting
and catching, and heard their talk, which was just like
mine. I heard the pitchers' fear of Yamaguchi, a great
lefthanded hitter. Often, he slammed balls
over the rightfielder's head clear to Eighth Street
and he could punch it to left when he took a notion.
Fujitani was a block of muscle behind the plate
in his armor that snicked and clunked as he worked.
He could whip off his mask, spring after a bunt
like a grasshopper, and fire to first or second
in one motion. Duncan Matsushita threw
heartbreaking curveballs that dropped suddenly
into the strike zone, and he seldom walked batters.
I began to cheer for my favorites. They laughed
that I could pronounce their names, no stranger to me
than the Deuteronomy, Malachi, Ecclesiastes
I'd been hearing all morning at church.

Water Pitcher

for J.G.

sixth grade miss curley showed a reproduction
Young Woman with a Water Pitcher
so full of light the opposite of sinister
i fell in love with jan vermeer's painting
as surely as i was in love with baseball
the next great lefthander for the st louis cardinals
in the wake of pollet, brecheen, and haddix
or johnny vandermeer of the reds
who pitched consecutive no-hitters one week in june
my brother said my fastball looked like
it was travelling through water   but i did
have a curve
               fifty years later at the national gallery
with love but no baseball career in my arm
i am thrilled by the real thing   i see his true name
on a page in the catalogue "johannes van der meer"
—johnny vandermeer!
was he a lefthander too, i wonder

And You, Gilbert Stuart

for Richard Rezac and Julia Fish

Sometimes it appears to be
all buying and selling:
at the capital
in the National Gallery
I stared
at the salmon-colored faces
of the first few Presidents
chanting of soap and water and beef
above foaming white collars and waistcoats
(again, with vague hope
of riddling the ambiguity of my citizenship)
locked as long as paintings last
in the legerdemain of your brush.

And now back home out West
I sit in my studio
before an empty canvas
thinking of Celilo, the dam-doomed falls
where men stood on rocks and logs
dipping nets, facing cold spray
in the red rays of their sinking day,
ellipsis to the long sentence
of their history
and the drowned future of their rights
(Power must be served)
and I think of Yakima
up the river
where a black boy
whose grandfather was born
the year of the Proclamation
loved schools
called Adams, Madison,
Jefferson, Washington. . .

Washington
the good slavemaster.
master of the minuet.
refuser of crowns,
surveyor of free ground
that he sold for many dollars.

And you, Gilbert Stuart,
painter of Presidents,
who they say had a habit
of reeling in suckers twice,
didn't The Great American Purchaser
sit for you
to begin the century on canvas?
And by 1805 weren't you still
dancing around his inquiries with the excuse
that you weren't satisfied with the painting?
And didn't you sell it
to the Fourth President?
(Whom you'd also painted, along with Dolly)
And didn't you finally, in 1821,
slip the old sage
a slick copy, purportedly the original
(His daughter remarked the wet paint),
on a mahogany panel?
(Canvas had been embargoed since 1801)
Oh yes you did.

Private Birdsong Speaks
(an excerpt)

I

at first i couldn't believe that people
needed to hear that stuff malcolm was saying,
such an unscientific and mythologically thin
demonization of white people.
me a stiff precise recent english major, i wondered
about that x device, seemed like comic book stuff.
seemed like people let their brains be vacuumed out
by a flashy style.   i couldn't believe
so many people got so excited about malcolm
even though i myself had said upon first experiencing
large groups of young black men from the south and east:
                                "These brothers
have been driven out of their minds, they'll believe
anything."   they seemed—in my conceit
and because they looked like me—
like beings caught up in the wildest most uncontrollable
downward self-mutilation ritual i'd ever seen.

fort bliss, texas, 1960: they hadn't seen any
smalltown western brothers like me either
in building 1013.   first time i'd ever lived
outside the pacific northwest:
                        bunked opposite the band
were mostly signal corps troops and truck drivers,
army laborers.   i heard the brothers among them thought
i was queer because i was in the band, company clerk,
sat in the office at a typewriter, played trumpet and piano,
fraternized with whites in the band and didn't
join their forays to the juarez whorehouses
(not that i shunned the houses).   i got all the
troop news in the area from my friend Alonzo
a clever brother from chicago who'd spent three years
at northwestern, who told me endless tales of that city

and about memphis where he'd lived earlier.   where
he witnessed a white policeman slap his aged father
for not addressing him as sir (his father had said, "Son,
I'm old enough to be your father," and then, bam! the cop
slapped him)

II

i learned the surrounding black troops considered the band
a white unit even though it contained an occasional black or more.
this didn't occur to me since i'd never been in any other kind
of class team or organization.   the band was peopled by
a cross-section of draftees and regular army maniacs
career juveniles alcoholics saints depressives and screwballs.
middle-aged men who needed uncle sammy
to provide them with a maze to run through or a boot in the ass
when they misbehaved—great stories—including il maestro himself,
mr tappendorff, a chief warrant officer of shaky baton who feared
virtuosos and terrorized the weak and uneducated.   who'd stop the music,
and scream, "Tucker, if you don't raise that goddam stand
so help me Christ, I'll court-martial you!"   oh yes he would and i swear
that around christmas his ravings became
increasingly loaded with angry jesuses christs sohelpmechrists
and forchristsakeses than usual
yeah, mr t was a white man but he wasn't about race.
he was unanimously about self-hate and misery.

III

take the time we went up to silver city new mexico.
the mexican girls up there went crazy over the white guys.
mean i wasn't looking for anything in particular but
my eligibility smarted a little bit.   anyhow it was a whistle stop
up in the mountains they say billy the kid used to haunt.
when we piled out of the bus
you'd have thought the glenn miller orchestra had hit town.
kids asking for autographs   girls throwing open their knees.

                    since the girls looked past me
i spent the time practicing my horn and smoking pot
with some of my buddies who thought they were too hip
for these here small-town chicks.
i remember sitting on a low stone wall at the edge
of a small college campus with my two best buddies
one from connecticut the other from massachusetts.
i think that was the night gilson said to me, "You're
pretty great, Birdie, but if you were from Boston
you'd be greater."
                              we inhaled the summer midnight
passing a joint around imagining we were philosophizing
on politics   the army   music   women
under the huge elm trees.   streetlights cut the dark
like blocks of yellow cheese.   our words took on interstellar
overtones. we said, "Heavy . . . yeah, heavy, man . . .
oh, man that's heavy."   At one point a woman
passed on the sidewalk across the street,
followed by a barking terrier.   one of the guys said,
"She's in her period. The dog can smell the blood."
heavy, man, beyond belief. . . .
                        our leader who made a career out of harassing
draftee privates spent his first evening in silver city
in the backseat of a carful of twenty-year-old
privates and high school girls getting drunk
and necking with sophomores and juniors.   the next day he was
his same old uptight miserable self of course.
i mean give me some relief, people!

Smell Theory

We hugged. Her thick black coat told
of fire, and the scent was in her hair
when she returned from the studio.
A tramp, to escape the cold snap, had no doubt
got into the lower part of the building
and built himself a little fire that prospered
too much, that alarmed the street before dawn,
smoked out the architects upstairs and
the mannikin shop and the artists above them.
One of the neighborhood homeless that roamed
below the lofts, perhaps a Nez Perce
from up the river, shivering here
ten thousand years later without trees
or family or animals under steel and concrete
that curb the river. Stiff, puffy guys with
cigarettes stuck to lips, trying to keep warm.
Maybe a woman with them. They've got coats
but this freeze feels big as the nation.

At the Jackson Pollock Retrospective in L.A.

Blue Poles, a long painting, mute, manic, American,
its tilted blue members looking strong as rebar
in the chaos they dominate, halted me and legions
of others open-mouthed, as if watching a dangerous
and fantastic aerial performance. All afternoon
I jostled back and forth between giant spattered
canvases. Lacy layered violence in the black and green
masterpiece once bartered for psychiatric help tore
at my schoolish fears. I floated back to my aunt's house
electrified, dreaming those brilliant splashes and drippings
from the wounded alcoholic. But crashed against
the drunken ghost of Uncle George, Aunt Martha's husband,
a tense umber ferret who disappeared for years at a time,
periodically spotted by cousins in St. Louis, Cleveland, Detroit,
or Los Angeles.
        I'd seen him once in person, years ago, looking
depressed and blinky. Mother had a picture of him
in uniform, standing at parade rest outside some tar-
papered Negro barracks. Now here he was, popped up in my face
at Aunt Martha's house. She barely got out, "This is Harold,
Lou's boy. He—" before he leapt into his monologue
about the war: That he was alive because the general,
a southerner, had liked the Negro unit's cooking,
and thus he hadn't had to cook under fire at the front
after the hell of amphibious landing. But he hadn't escaped shock,
or alcohol. He sat there rocking to the progress
of whiskey and war through his heart. An ill wind—
I fought to hang on to the lamppost of my painting dream.
He slapped me on the kneecap—"Do ya hear me, boy!"
—with the back of his hand. War blazed before
his bloodshot eyes, and his voice boiled into my ears.
                        He created the whistle of incoming
mortars, uprooted orchards in torn black soil, windfall
apples scattered like flung beads of red and yellow

paint under zinc-tasting smoke. Some boys from Alabama
got wasted in a jeep with a colored captain and a boy
from Memphis who could play the saxophone . . . boxes
with their names stacked in a corner of a chilly hangar.
he showed how he used to prop his teeth open
with his dogtags to test the notch because he was sure
he was going to bite some o' that sombitchin' French dust—
"That's a long way from Yakima, ain't it, boy," he shouted,
backhanding my knee and fuming the air 'til my eyes watered.
But that cracker general had liked his cooking
and he'd lived. "You don't think that's somethin'?"
                        He tried to shake his head into comprehension,
shuddered, rocked, and cursed me for not being
a sport like Virgil, my twin brother, who armed him
with a bottle whenever they met. Then he veered back
to the war, staring bug-eyed into France, blue lips worming,
grey hair frozen straight up like one sitting terrified
piloting his gravebox.

Pat Ware

The focus is loss. As Pat Ware puts it, "Most of the poems just formed as reactions to losses, not only important people and family, but the farm itself, and an awful need for things that don't die per se." How does the writing help? The poems "are therapeutic and seem to exorcise the darkness that was so much part of those times." Ware often locates these poems in a farming landscape. "One of the main influences, and often the grounds for the poems, is the culture of farming. I was partially reared on my Italian grandparents' farm, and then in 1970 I had a farm of my own" (in Long Beach, Washington). The poems started elsewhere. "After a trip to Mexico with my dog in 1975 I came home with a passion to write." Next came a workshop at Portland State University with Primus St. John. "He was enormously encouraging." St. John brought William Stafford to class. "His poems were spiritually present for me, but also relational without agony or confusion. His was a voice I could love." On to Centrum in Pt. Townsend, Washington. "Horrible experiences in some ways, but absolutely necessary for development and connection to the writing community." And much reading of poets Roethke, Bogan, Hugo, Sexton, Bishop, and Gallagher. Ware is also a painter and graphic artist, and works for a mental health organization in Portland, where she lives.

Death, the Helium Eye

Death is a dream; it shades the heart.
Its rattle grins me, ear to ear.
I shake when we're together or apart.

I go into the world but make no mark.
Time passes me, how can I say where?
Death is a dream, it shades the heart.

I see well and yet this way is dark.
Are you here? Stay right where you are.
I shake when we're together or apart.

This love is under perish from the start.
I feel its hand in everything I fear.
Death is a dream. It shades the heart.

The planet cracks. Who will wake
me from this dream we both have dared?
I shake if we're together or apart.

Dark bleeds in my elbow, light is dark.
But open as an eyelid you come near.
Death is a dream, it shades the heart.
I shake when we're together or apart.

Permission for Autopsy

This will enable you to make an examination.
Notice the butt of the chin,
how it rears, pulling against the reins
of the halter. Make it
lie down and roll for you: the soft
entrails can be pulled aside
with just the right cut, and then
you must elevate the heart.
It is already dead of course,
just ease in your hands where the warm
pools are going black: this is the source
of the trouble, a failure
to recognize the creature was a runner.
Notice how the limbs even now
are twitching and flick up to catch
the sun along the silver feet.
Don't hesitate to press hard,
this will contract the muscle, shooting
blood like a bullet from its brain.
As a doctor you can wish it to come alive
even after the last shocks
sucked you into opening more
of the chest. The dream is wise
that sees you riding it down
to a small stream, smaller even
as the veins grow smaller, and you know
there is no wisdom for horses.
Just as there cannot be running,
even in dark days, without a heart.

Obligations of Solitude

All the way home to the beach
in the empty seat beside me
I hear the troubles of the dead.

Rhythm thumps in and out
with the view, a beat breaks down
into tires and mileposts.

Firs stripe by. Sky white
and spaced, I lose myself to
speed, drive this road hoping

home is halfway to my heart
with a rebate on unpaid rent.
Fools are not around this bend.

I see stirrup tops
of firs: they hold the true
direction and it's not up

but in, they ask me to take.
The hamlet greens of May,
their sun pools of molten ore

renew my eyes. Dimmed all the way
to black when I
wake myself again, I pull on the wheel

and count down the last ten miles.
The door is stuck but opens,
the chairs facing me
with their arms.

Long Beach, September at the Sea Horse, 1978

Heat beams sharpen their crystal tongues at dawn
On empty streets electric outlines hum

Those breakers, like white carnations
The sweet dismay of the carousel, breeze turned

Toy cars with bent antennae, the dark cockpits
Huddled like wooden shoes on the glossy floor

While across the rocks a crab gathers
And settles its legs, seagulls mewing overhead

The glitter of glasses through a tavern door
A shadow climbing a stool, a woman wiping the bar

The grayness of street, the colorless fog
Rolling: no odor, no taste, no sound

Trawlers tiny enough to see, ocean and cloud
in layers of soft geometry

Cul de sacs of grass, walkways butting against sand
The dun dunes snoozing like animals

Between the violin of lock and key
The wind gets in and stirs the fire

Words that rise, with no end, senseless
A slack tide changing bronze foam for land

Cries that are birds and cries that are people
The harping of flocks, the flocking of tourists

The coast hills on good days, blue boughs
Reminiscent of cloud, loaded with gale and squall

Pilings of an extinct quarantine dock
Encode the marsh with dots and dashes

Their dark rings mark a high tide line
Where water is lapping, and never ceases.

An Apostle's Greed

O Lord, of what I have done
and what I have failed to do,
the stomach alone knows the aches.
In this greed, a poet of second
helpings, fat as helium
ascends to face you.
Gourmet hopes blend toast
and honey, as here I take the host
and pretend, oh holy the faces
I wear today. Yet internally
I ask all the angels and saints
and you in your maternity,
to teach me mad restraint.
Water, Lord have mercy, water,
Christ have mercy. End with tears
upon what really matters,
upon what really matters
let there be tears of real water.

Listening to Distance

In the firm line, past the pale
row of houses I can imagine
the ocean, steaming and sleeping
in its rockery of old continents.
Traffic floats from
the city its thin punishment
of gray: tires, diesels,
and a preferential rain falls.

Ships I've never known
pierce the last bank of cloud
thick in their colonies of freight,
deep in profits we'll never see.

It is moonless here too.
And you, beyond eye level,
in countries grown close
by weak economy, what legions
fill your minds, your needs?

Do you wake and feel time
rushing in, drumming on the streets?
Leaders announce, weapons
cocked to the approach of intruder.
The sound of war
steady in its losses, causes
you to stare at the one horizon.

It is moonless here too.
I look over roof to that other darkness,
the thought of you
looking back,

want you to find
which wisp from where you stand
is the smoke my city makes,
and think of me peering and watching
the flat light fall in the east.

Calling Out Light

Silver-eyed, the calf is half rubber.
His nose and lip thud on the gate.
He pumps the cow's full udder,

eyes swimming in the black lake
of birth. He runs, he runs out
the first day, bawling at grass, awake

in the flurry of the new-born proud.
And nothing moves to him
but his mother, her swung bag and stout

tongue. An ember in the east is dim:
does he see before sun,
moon, the rivers that tear out of men,

the light in his carnal origin?

Immolation

He lit himself with a match
and instantly the pain
came in streaks on his face,
till pain was water
in its livid magma brilliance
and he crumpled to his seat
gently as a doll,
lightly bouncing. The mouth
half-opened in an O was breathing,
oh, the same as eyes & fingers,
the navel
coursing in its net
of flames, as they took
the center. Once he nearly raised
from the ground on blue
wings of color, intense as words
have no voice
in the crackling, his back
drawing a light line
in the swimming atmosphere,
and he went down,
first at the shoulders, head
tilted slightly, and slowly
falling forward, as
the man's coals
brightened and turned
the long-awaited gray.

Flukefish

The base of its spine is a throat,
mucous-packed. No word gets out.
I dream backbone, fish.
Bright sea.
I fear no bone, unheralded
rock, to swim
becomes flag the way it sways.

Here for fillet
I spin, torqued to fishhook
till even pain
waves everywhere but down.

Fluke face, manta,
why so flat? inside the good
flesh you inhabit,
the sensible shark, the black whale.

I turn you
and fly at you with whips,
knives for which you pray
scan your hide.

The dog comes,
its teeth filled with weed.
Roll over, free your face.
Drown your belly in white.

The Loner

Your eyes don't fool me,
they move in.
They close.
I live where I cannot see
a single human house.
Sky and field is all.
Let someone else
live where there is hazard.
Let them stock up
on food, fuel engines
with expensive oils.
Neighbors spy
behind the leaves
of my cabin, figuring
they'll make out who I am.
They don't know, I see them.
At night their lights go on below:
they do this to walk in the dark.
Their streets wake up
and roll, conveyor belts
move people from place to place.
I can tell
you about those belts, they're hidden.
Just as underneath
my floor there's a leaf,
cold and dry on the earth,
year in and out. It stays.
Those belts are a purpose.
I search my home
for a pot, a can, a winter brush:
because I own this place.
They want me down
to chat and dance.
Vital supplies are all
I need, not propaganda.
Not someone else's wife.

The Window Over the St. Vincent Garden

Your face broke like a green shell
and the creature left with an echo
from your mouth. This is the imagined
terrapin, or rasping gecko I saw
escape the white room when you died.

It made the garden where the low
fountain washes the feet of St. Vincent.

Staring out, I absorb the pounding
of their hands on your chest, bed
lurching under the haunted weight. Below

me, limbs weep in shimmering strings
to clear the clotted drops—
lilac and azalea smear to color.

I whisper your favorite
rhododendron names and remember
none of them but Sappho, her love

for beauty, the sound of beauty.
I have nothing else to think of here,
waiting for the sound to go away.

Theresa

If anyone asks, it is the house,
alive in the foothills of the city
that is mine
crazed though I am about time,
the decades of remembered rooms
in eyes that could not see.

Say it's the metal surface of clouds,
the wealth of watercress
suddenly lush in the icy creek,
when fall comes, that reminds me of you.

or your hand on the bedrail, yellow
and swollen with death, as stacks of cells
gathered their water. . .

tell me you are alive
and see the scorching sunrise hit the woods,
make lanterns of bush and bark, trails
of thought where shadows blanket;

where shadow has gone, tell me
you are cooking
this Sunday, like hundreds of Sundays
when men and fields came in, and hunger
flew in Italian idioms,
the pungence of tomato and cheese
strong as language.

Disguised in these swirling leaves is
an autumn wheel where you are dancing,
that shun eyes from light
we cannot see,

while there on the kitchen floor
thousands of spring seeds roll to the walls
and I want to plant them
with your hands.

How Deep is the Garden?

One day time will leave me.
I'll know gray smoke,
like intelligence it will vanish.
My mind then attached to trees
will silently ponder earth,
round as eyes lost in the distance.

One day the family I wanted
will rattle at the door as I
wait, included as a shadow.
The things I know and do not know
will be given away.

In a house like this black one,
I see a chip of land only,
and am stunned by the love of death.
I strive in heart and mind
to hold these sorrows like strangers,
and make it home to the land
where there is no air.

Carolyn Miller

Ragtime, quadratic equations, and the poetry of Antonio Machado are among the constellation of Carolyn Miller, whose great grandmother homesteaded in Walla Walla, Washington in 1857. There, Miller was raised. She spent summers in the Blue Mountains of Oregon, and went on to American University, where she graduated summa cum laude in mathematics. In Salem, Oregon, Miller taught high-school mathematics and, with her husband, raised a family. In 1978, she looked into poetry. She has since taken workshops from Richard Hugo, David Wagoner, Maxine Kumin, Madeline DeFrees, Sandra McPherson, Chris Howell, and Peter Sears. At these workshops she met all but one of the poets in this anthology. She has found that "Writing is a way to keep the world in focus, walk around it, keep it present and new." Miller has read her poetry on KBOO radio and at the Portland Poetry Festival. She has taught for the Oregon Writers Workshop and won the Helen Bullis Prize from *Poetry Northwest.* A favorite poem of hers is X.J. Kennedy's "Little Elegy." "Language invents us," Miller writes, "and we reciprocate by making songs, stories, poems. We get a finite time to consider the world, the difference being we have to do both the noticing and remembering on the fly, and there's no candy bar at the end."

The Curved Lens of Forgetting

When Mother died, I broke my glasses
and wore her bifocals. They made me dizzy.
She was having trouble inhaling
so they gave her Demerol, which depresses
the breath, I don't understand that.
She struggled for hours, unable to ask

why last summer when Dad's lung collapsed
the doctor accidentally punctured the other
and the machine breathing for him refused to work
and the nurse prepared a huge morphine injection
to stop the moaning—
the sky turned green, the sky turned yellow—

if I don't write this what will connect me?
I've taken everything I can from the summer cabin:
mildew'd wicker, the ice box, the rickety
fireset, Grandmother's treadle with the starflower
drawer pulls, a telephone table from the year
we stopped being primitive.

Each time I go back, Dad's on the roof
in Sunday trousers, with a bundle of shingles.
Mother scolds from the porch step, fingers flaking
Crisco and flour. They're younger than I am.
Room by room, Dad chases until he tags, Mother wheels
inches shorter, arms reaching. They stand
one body, pressed together like hot weather flowers.

Someday they'll reach down and pick me up, saying
who are you?

The Girl Who Loved Groceries

When her weight-trainer shouts
    "What ya got—muscle between the ears?"
when the soul food man yells
    she has brains like chitterlings
when a physicist, under pressure,
    makes her dense or vacuous
    according to whim
she admits
    bad luck in men.

If she decides to love a writer from *Field
and Stream,* will she babble whenever
the conversation goes over his head?
If she marries a dentist, will he say
"Your brain, like an unfilled cavity,
rings hollow," or something less formal?
At least he might use novocaine.
Twice a year, he'd give her mouth
his full attention, his hands
cool and gentle, and later,
he'd prescribe something for the pain.

On blind dates, she asks his career
and prepares for the metaphor—
it makes a game of disagreements.
Will a projectionist find her
a dim bulb, back on the last reel?

A girl gets single-
minded: she wants to be right.
Nights, admiring aisles of a grocery
she watches the boy arrange tomatoes, the can man
respectfully bend to the click of her heels.
Tender, how green smocks
stop restocking shelves as she passes,
the box boy lifting a look of esteem.

She is dreaming:
they wave from their aprons.
The butcher steps blamelessly
forward, his hands colorful and damp.
He smiles, simply because she rang,
the customer is always
dizzy from hunger.
Barechested to save her shirt,
she's falling all over his big red heart.

Fugue in Green

Every day the furred green worm inside
warming the chrysalis
works out with weights
His last thrust
could light up a forest
        la luna vampira
          sexual on flowers

So spring comes crowbar and bloom
So spring comes tipping the fir trees
turpentine green

        You're growing up the gray doctor said
        his hands leafed out
        twigging her branches
What could she ask
dumbbell, decibel-clumsy

why boys are taller than seaweed
and given to one-handed steering?
why they follow a green noise tires make
        against pavement
why their mouths are thistlegrin
        a girl's two-fingered whistle

———

Piccolo green, he pulled her down
a kiss for a penny
She heard the copperhead clink

        She wants green smoke, green silk
        a ring if
        the moon had a finger

———

Ocean floor, mother of green
scattered with shark's teeth
gravity lives where nothing can crush it
neither the wolf eel   nor lord turtle
humped over the murkhole

His touch was fresher than haycock
green than grapple

Plumb bob, green nail
she in carapace, he in green armor
unfold a house made of hinges
Spring's slow motion stem
enters the bung-hole

maidenhair, stag fern, applegreen gash
worm in the apple   she remembers
the fig tree
        didn't give a good green dam

———

Dressing; undressing, spring comes dicotyledon
back and forth across fields, lime-green

hypnofixing leafhopper beetles
buzzing clover's green swarm

It enters old men and sends them whacking
They lean on its wickerwood cane
because the world is in meadow

What to do with boyish clamor
a woman's evergreen body?

The moon is shoehorn green!
moonmaple slips at the window, wands

that buckle the knee or make the legs shaky
so lovers lie down for the drummer's green brush
———

Wrap-around, the skirt had a certain
hollyhock flair that couldn't be hobbled

Even dressed in curmudgeon/crabstick/crosspatch
green would bob October for apples

      This is desire   a crone   prong green
      from the horny toad of submission
      could break her cudgel
      twitching for water
      the smell of green roses

Salt Lick

Clearly she has the gift
    of beardstongue and adder
        When he tasted her eyelids

he felt so tongue and groovy
    night came lollygagging out of the puddle
        fugue for a frog

unrolling the princess
    her golden yarn   Oh
        her hair yellow as tung oil

So they stood honeybeard in the iris
    he gazing up as if a perfect fly
        might fall from the moony tip of her clapper

like human lovers, he thought, whose eyes stop
    though their mouths play on, the flautist
        coaxing gamelan shiver

Henceforth he will walk in oxblood cordovans
    tongue-tied and flapping
        because she promised to share a bed

Or was she speaking tongue in cheek
    she of the shrew   pickled
        saucy, hardbitten, suddenly calling out *Froglegs?*

calling *You squid-red lick of a rascal*
    (Bite her mother tongue angel
        death in the molars)

Wounded, he ties up his slivered calf
    his jellied lamb's   foot-in-the-moccasin
        and shuts his green maw

He's lower than a tongue depressor—
    he who has taken a thousand flymaids
        buckle-tongue through the eyelet!

Ah, his heart is a salt lick
    brine the moon rolls in
        with no one to fetch it

Ma Bête

It must be a spell, so much ugliness
a castle grew up around it, twenty-foot walls.
A curse to rule over: brutes live alone
with terrible faces, and only fresh young hearts
can improve their appearance.

At first he stood in her doorway only in shadow,
or through the garden, he let her glimpse his separate path
until she could look without flinching.
So weeks later, when dusk sprang at them,
they stood still as two harts in different sorrows.
In different sorrows, they watched the clouds go cold.
Of course he asked, but she wouldn't.
She bawled for her father.

> Why should he care for her puny skin?
> Hasn't he given her jewels and a magic mirror to play in?
> Instead she spends her day digging among roots
> in the garden, a rodent not fit to be his food.

Every evening, through his roses, she will not marry him.
Vapor from his nostrils envelops her head,
she curves her palm over his gloomy paw and they walk
along the parapet. When she leans into his fur,
when she looks up with quizzy eyes, he wants to be human
with ten harmless fingers. He's not allowed to tell the charm,
so he cheats, makes her dream *The Frog and the Prince*.

> What if she will have him and it isn't true
> about the spell, what if she will, and they go on forever
> waiting for that transformation?
> And what does it matter: she is all bony elbows,
> a hollow at the base of his throat.

    Could he spend a lifetime watching her eat things
    already dead? He won't shed his russet pelt,
    handsome as foxskins he rips in his private wood.
    And she has taken to calling him *ma Bête*. Is it a joke
    to have his face so ugly, to have fur in his mouth?
    And he is weary from balancing two legs against his tail.

Every night he sleeps in different directions
so she, stumbling lonely, will not catch him by surprise.
He might take her for a snowrabbit and tear her belly.
Tonight the very room he chooses without reason
she hides in, weeping. He must stop and listen.
It is like the moon's rain falling into his heart.
When he takes hold of the door, he is shocked by grief
in the silver knob. Through his hide
he sees her lying frail as a broken bird
and naked. She will not know when he enters,
her face a velvet mask
on which she has painted
the face of a beast.

Piscatorial Longing

I can't tell one from another flowering—
    peach, almond or cherry.
How to get back to the bud, stop
    the face dividing,
    the spiny unbuckling,
    human eyes adrift under the lids' migration.
        A tail flashes, gone.
From birth, life is
    the body rushing away.
        We visit the old, and as we walk away
        we become them.

Teach me to sway in the shallows
    where all are rooted
        moon and boulder,
        gray man, lemony woman.
    A stillness connects us
    longing deep under the bone.
We want what animals hunted in tribes before speech:
    comfort, food, safety from falling.
Is that what love is
    primitive belly?
    The maple tree outside my window sprouting
        chartreuse beaks and yellow feathers

wants, wants
the hour before daylight, I know
it has less taste for love than passion,
    I feed it *shipwreck*
    I feed it *lonely oar asleep on the river*
    I feed it.

Spinning

At fifteen a girl has trouble
sleeping.
        She shook
        half-awake, the mask
        spinning down toward her mouth
        sprouting rib-wings and the legs of a spider
        slipped lower,
        the round belly rounder
        and bigger and nearer,
until she screamed
and leapt up to sit all night in a wing chair,
her wide eyes surrounded.
It was her soul wanting in
to be the soul of a woman.

        Lights on, search the ceiling,
        the baseboards, shake out the quilts.
        Where does it hide
        where does it hover
        spidery heart
        deep under cover?

Old women tell, or tell nothing.
Why frighten a girl into the shape of a woman
carried over a lintel: terror
        as good marries evil
        the knight devours the maiden, the innocent
        lays her head in the serpent's lap.

A while she refused it
ate less and less, her arms and legs
spider thin.
        "Not me," she said
        to the wind and the weather,
                this bone of my bone
                this flesh of my river.

Falling Forward into Light

—Long ago, we learned to want, and walk away.—

1
The neighbor has walked out of his
dark doorway, and the big-breasted woman
who visits him shows her hair yellow
under the streetlamp. They are old.
They walk, settling first on one side,
then the other. Weighty matters

under the moon's anchor. I have
come out of my house, pulled by stone
the moon burning dust. At the curb
he stutters, *sorry, sorry,*
until I am breathless
looking into white azaleas. Stars

that wait to break our bodies
wake from the past. How softly
they speak to each other, all lost
in the trees. I hope he tells her
nothing. It is spring
and dying will explain itself.

2
All night an owl calls true
in the deathhouse of petals,
where half the world sleeps standing
to avoid the touch. Beautiful dream:
to dream our bodies slump forward
and the masks fall.

3
Starlings worry my tree with morning
shadows. They tell what they can

and will not repeat themselves. *Only,*
they sing, and climb through their stations
into utter silence. They have flown up
in their darkest contours,
wings around stars.
The sky has moved beyond me
and I let it go. They will carry it back
like a petal, pale and pale
over the hills, a spreading smoke.
Has the neighbor seen dawn lit with sparrows,

how they flick through the branches
drumming their feathers? Perhaps the woman
winked back her despair, perhaps
he is kissing her, leaning forward
over his big belly, as the last birds
cry out in the yellow tulips.

Credits

SUSAN SPADY

The poems in this anthology first appeared in the following magazines: "Flower Leaning from a Vase," "Underpants" in *CALYX*; "Practice This Ending" in *Cimarron Review*; "The Wishing Pool" in *Fireweed*; "Bruised," "Carrying Eggs," "A Room of One's Own," "Rock Paper Scissors" in *Poetry Northwest*.

VICTORIA WYTTENBERG

The poems in this anthology first appeared in the following magazines : "House for Sale" in *G.W. Review*; "For My Oldest Child" in *Malahat Review*; "Flowers Have Beauty and Roots Have Worth" in *Poetry Canada*; "The School Photographer," "Imprecations Against Adultery," "Bird Shadows," "The Curse" in *Poetry Northwest*; "Blue Heron" in *Seattle Review*.

CHARLES GOODRICH

The poems in this anthology first appeared in the following magazines: "The Insects of South Corvallis" in *Fireweed*; "Hover Fly" in *The Fishtrap Anthology*; "Heavenly Bodies in *Flight: A Poetry Anthology*; "Stinging Nettles" in *Zyzzyva*; "Millennial Spring" in *Orion*.

BARBARA DAVIS

The poems in this anthology first appeared in the following magazines : "Conversations in the Dark" in *The Chadakoin Review*; "Chamberwork for the Eighth Day" in *Northwest Poets & Writers Calendar*; "In the Garden of the Women" in *Visions International*; "Paper Nautilus" in *The Worcester Review*.

DEBRA BRIMACOMBE

This is Debra Brimacombe's first publication.

HAROLD JOHNSON

The poems in this anthology first appeared in the following magazines: "The Names of Summer," "Smell Theory," "Jackson Pollock Retrospective" in *Fireweed*.

PAT WARE

The poems in this anthology first appeared in the following magazines: "Immolation" in *Moose Magazine;* "Window over the St. Vincent Garden" in the contest publication of The Oregon State Poetry Association; "Permission for Autopsy" in *Willamette Week*.

CAROLYN MILLER

The poems in this anthology first appeared in the following magazines: "The Girl Who Loved Groceries" in *Fine Madness;* "Falling Forward into Light" in *Ironwood;* "Fugue in Green" in *Left Bank;* "The Curved Lens of Forgetting" in *The Malahat Review;* "Ma Bête" in *Poetry Northwest*.

About the editors and artists

PETER SEARS, co-editor, came to Oregon in 1974 to teach creative writing at Reed College, and worked for 11 years at the Oregon Arts Commission. He now works at *Rubberstampmadness* and lives in Corvallis with his wife, Anita Helle. He is the 1999 winner of the Peregrine Smith Poetry Contest. His previous book of poems is *Tour, New & Selected Poems* from Breitenbush Books. He has also published books on teaching from Scholastic Inc. and Teachers & Writers Collaborative.

MICHAEL MALAN, co-editor, is the author of a chapbook, *The Steak Palace & Other Poems,* and a book, *Distant Laughter.* He has studied poetry writing with A. R. Ammons and Robert Morgan at Cornell, and with Dennis Schmitz at Sacramento State University. Michael is managing editor of *Rubberstampmadness,* a magazine for rubber stamp artists and collectors.

ANN STALEY, associate editor, co-founded, with Eric Muller, the poetry magazine *Fireweed*. She has recently retired from teaching writing and literature in Oregon high schools, and is associate faculty at the Northwest Writing Institute at Lewis and Clark College in Portland, Oregon.

NANCY CLARK designed this book. She paints in many media, including pastel, pencil, and watercolor. Nancy is the art director at *Rubberstampmadness.*

VALERIE BESSER created the cover art. She is an art director and illustrator in Paris.